21st Century Skills Library

LIFE SKILLS BIOGRAPHIES

ROBERTO CLEMENTE

Vicky Franchino

Cherry Lake Publishing
Ann Arbor, Michigan

Published in the United States of America by Cherry Lake Publishing
Ann Arbor, MI
www.cherrylakepublishing.com

Content Adviser: Bruce Markusen, Author and Historian, Cooperstown, New York

Photo Credits: Cover and pages 1, 5, 6, 8, 9, 10, 12, 14, 16, 18, 20, 22, 25, 26, 29, 31, 32, 34, 35, 36, 43, © Bettmann/Corbis; page 13, © Lucien Aigner/Corbis; page 38, Photo courtesy of the National Baseball Hall of Fame and Museum; page 41, © Tannen Maury/ epa/Corbis

Library of Congress Cataloging-in-Publication Data
Franchino, Vicky.
  Roberto Clemente / by Vicky Franchino.
    p. cm.—(Life skills biographies)
  Includes bibliographical references.
  ISBN-13: 978-1-60279-073-5 (hardcover)
  ISBN-10: 1-60279-073-6 (hardcover)
  1. Clemente, Roberto, 1934–1972—Juvenile literature. 2. Baseball players—Puerto Rico—
Biography—Juvenile literature. I. Title. II. Series.
  GV865.C45F73 2007
  796.357092–dc22
    [B]   2007004443

Cherry Lake Publishing would like to acknowledge the work of
The Partnership for 21st Century Skills.
Please visit www.21stcenturyskills.org *for more information.*

Contents

INTRODUCTION

Baseball players are usually remembered for their athletic skills. Roberto Clemente is one baseball star whose accomplishments off the field were just as important as those on it.

A professional baseball player for nearly 20 years, Clemente had an impressive list of achievements. He was only the 11th player in the Major Leagues to have 3,000 hits in his career. He helped his team, the Pittsburgh Pirates, win the World Series twice, and he received 12 consecutive Gold Glove Awards for fielding. But when people hear his name today, they remember more than a baseball player. They remember a man of great dignity who worked to gain equality for Latino ballplayers—and Latino people—a man who cherished his Puerto Rican heritage, and a man who knew it was important to help others.

As Clemente once said, "Any time you have an opportunity to make a difference in this world and you don't, then you are wasting your time on Earth."

CHAPTER ONE

LIFE IN PUERTO RICO

Cutting sugarcane, as Roberto Clemente's father did, is a physically demanding job.

Roberto Clemente Walker was born on August 18, 1934, in Carolina, Puerto Rico. (In the Puerto Rican tradition, his mother's maiden name is given last.) His parents were Luisa and Melchor Clemente, and Roberto had five older brothers and two older sisters. Both of Roberto's parents worked at a sugarcane plantation. Luisa did laundry for the owner of the plantation. She started her job in the middle of the night so that she could be home to care for her children during the day. Melchor cut sugarcane and eventually became a foreman and supervised other workers. He often held more than one job to support his family. Sometimes Melchor ran a grocery store out of his house, and other times he used the family truck to make deliveries. These were difficult jobs that paid very little, but Roberto's parents did them gladly in order to take care of their family.

Although much of Roberto's time was spent helping his family, there was always time for play. His favorite game to play was baseball. There wasn't usually enough money to buy bats and balls, but that didn't stop Roberto. He would make a bat from a tree branch and a ball from a tin can, and spend hours playing. When he wasn't playing baseball, he was listening to it on the radio or riding his bike to Sixto Escobar Stadium in the nearby city of San Juan. There he would wait patiently in hopes of seeing one of the baseball stars as they left the stadium. His favorite player was Monte Irvin. Irvin played for the **Negro Leagues** during the regular baseball season in the United States and for the San Juan team—the Senators—during the **Winter League** (which was

Through their actions, Luisa and Melchor Clemente taught their son valuable lessons about hard work, sacrifice, and the importance of helping others. They worked long hours and sometimes went without food so that their children wouldn't be hungry. They taught Roberto that every person was equal, regardless of skin color or wealth.

held there because the weather in Puerto Rico is mild enough to play baseball outdoors year-round). Sometimes Roberto would wait at the stadium in the hopes of seeing his favorite player, and eventually he was brave enough to ask Irvin for his autograph. The two became friends and were often together at the stadium. Little did they guess that Roberto would one day become a major league baseball player and have the chance to play against his longtime hero!

Roberto's hometown of Carolina, Puerto Rico, is about 13 miles (21 kilometers) from San Juan (above), the island's largest city, which is on the coast.

When he was young, Roberto asked his father for a bicycle. His father told him that he'd have to find a way to earn money for the bike, and so Roberto did. Each morning, he hauled a heavy can of milk for a neighbor and received a few pennies in pay. It took him nearly three years to save his money, but he kept working until he had earned his bike.

Monte Irvin, who played for the New York Giants in the Major Leagues, also played in the Winter Leagues in Puerto Rico.

Roberto's parents wanted their children to have an easier life than they had. They knew Roberto loved baseball, but his mother believed that education was the best way to have a better life. Roberto was a fine

Playing on a Winter League team, such as the San Juan Senators, was a popular way for Major League players to hone their skills in the off season.

student, but it was obvious that baseball was more important to him than school. Luisa sometimes got upset that Roberto spent so much of his time playing baseball. Once she even threw his bat into the fire. Luckily, he was able to save his bat before it was completely destroyed. His mother later said that she had made a mistake when she tried to stop him from playing ball.

As a teenager, Roberto continued to spend all his free time practicing and playing baseball. A man named Roberto Marín came to watch him play.

Marín was a salesman who was in charge of finding players for his company's softball team. Once he saw how well Roberto could play, Marín asked him to join his team. Roberto was just 14 years old, and within two years he was also playing for the Juncos, a baseball team in the Puerto Rican Double-A League. To top it off, Roberto was still playing for his high school baseball team and was a star on the track team. In fact, Roberto was so good at track-and-field events that he was seriously considered for Puerto Rico's 1952 Summer Olympic team! But baseball was his favorite sport, and Roberto decided to dedicate himself to being the best baseball player he could be.

People often describe Roberto as the best natural athlete they ever saw, but he was also one of the hardest working. Even as a young boy, Roberto understood that it took time and effort to excel at something. He often carried a small rubber ball with him that he would squeeze to make his arms and hands stronger. He spent hours practicing his hitting, fielding, and throwing.

CHAPTER TWO

A LIFE IN BASEBALL BEGINS

Roberto's career in baseball began before he graduated from high school.

After watching Roberto play for nearly four years, Marín knew that the teen had enough talent to play professional baseball. Marín spoke to his friend, Pedrín Zorrilla, who was the owner of a popular Winter League team, the Santurce Cangrejeros. Many of the Winter League players were young men who wanted a chance to show their skills. The league was also popular with experienced players from the Major Leagues and the Negro Leagues in the United States who wanted to keep in shape during the off-season and earn some extra money.

Zorrilla also helped scout new players for the Brooklyn Dodgers baseball team in the United States. He invited Roberto to attend a tryout

The Newark Eagles played in the Negro Leagues in the United States in the 1930s and 1940s.

The Brooklyn Dodgers, who played at Ebbets Field in New York City, were one of the best teams in the Major Leagues in the mid-1950s. They won the World Series in 1955.

that was being held for the Cangrejeros and the Dodgers. This was an exciting opportunity for Roberto because Al Campanis would be there. Campanis was the Dodgers' head scout for **Latin American** talent. Campanis wasn't expecting much from the tryouts because they were open to everyone, not just talent found through his scouts.

Seventy-two hopeful players showed up for tryouts. At first, things went poorly, just as Campanis had expected. He didn't see anyone good enough to play professional baseball. But then it was Roberto's turn. He threw a ball from home plate to center field. His throw was fast and perfect. Campanis asked for *uno más*, or "one more," and this one was perfect, too. Then Roberto ran the 60-yard dash in just 6.4 seconds—the world record at the time was 6.1 seconds. And he ran uno más in the same time. Campanis was suddenly glad he'd attended the tryouts.

Campanis wanted to sign Roberto to the Brooklyn Dodgers right away, but there was one problem. According to the rules of Major League Baseball, a player had to be at least 18 years of age before he could sign a contract. Roberto was only 17.

The Puerto Rican league didn't have this rule, however, so Campanis's loss was Zorrilla's gain. Zorrilla offered Roberto a $400 bonus and a salary of $40 per week to play for the Cangrejeros. This was a fortune to Roberto and his family—his father was paid much less for his hard work at the plantation. Roberto discussed the offer with his parents. They knew how much this opportunity meant to him and agreed that he could sign on with the Cangrejeros.

The Cangrejeros' manager, Buster "Buzz" Clarkson, told Clemente that he'd be a great player someday, but he needed to improve his batting skills. When he batted, he dragged his left foot and would swing at almost every pitch, leaving him with a poor batting average. Clemente took Clarkson's advice and diligently worked to improve his batting. He became an excellent batter, winning four batting titles during his professional career.

On the Cangrejeros, Clemente played with Willie Mays (right).

Clemente was thrilled to play on a Winter League team. It would be his first chance to play against Major League players from the United States, and he was determined to do his best. But his excitement soon turned to frustration when he found himself spending most of his time on the bench. Zorrilla believed that young players could easily be discouraged if they played against experienced professional ballplayers and didn't do well. He thought these players would do better in the long run if they spent their early days on the team practicing and learning.

Clemente was upset when he didn't get to play, but he didn't let that stop him from working hard and learning all he could. His hard work eventually paid off, and he became the Cangrejeros' regular right fielder. He shared the outfield with two excellent ballplayers: Bob Thurman, who'd long been a star in the Negro Leagues, and Willie Mays, who played for the New York Giants. Playing with these talented and experienced men helped Clemente to become an even better ballplayer—and the scouts began to notice him.

The Brooklyn Dodgers had been keeping an eye on Clemente and wanted to sign him to the team. In 1954, they offered him a $10,000 bonus, plus a $5,000 salary. He couldn't believe his good fortune. He could earn more money than he'd ever dreamed of, playing the game that he loved. Plus he'd get to play with the Dodgers, one of the most famous teams in baseball. But before he actually signed the contract, the Milwaukee Braves approached him with a much higher offer. He couldn't decide what to do and turned to his mother for advice. She told him that it was important to keep his word, and he signed with the Brooklyn Dodgers.

Clemente was excited to join a Major League team. He knew that he was playing not only for himself, but for all the people of Puerto Rico.

Clemente adapted to varied roles and responsibilities throughout his career and excelled in them. He took being a role model to Puerto Rican children especially seriously. He remembered when he was a child, people always said, "Babe Ruth was the best there was. They said you'd really have to be something to be like Babe Ruth. But Babe Ruth was an American player. What we needed was a Puerto Rican player they could say that about, someone to look up to and try to equal." When he played baseball, Clemente knew that he was playing as a representative of all Puerto Rican people.

CHAPTER THREE

THE UPS AND DOWNS OF LIFE IN PROFESSIONAL BASEBALL

Jackie Robinson (crossing home plate), who was the first African American to play in the Major Leagues, played for the Montreal Royals in 1946.

Although Clemente had signed with the Dodgers, he was sent to play for their **farm team**, the Montreal Royals. Clemente was a talented right fielder, but the Dodgers already had all the outfielders they needed on their team. Most people believe the Dodgers signed him because they recognized his talent and wanted to keep their **rival**, the New York Giants, from getting him. But some people believe that Clemente was sent to Montreal because there were already many players of color on the Dodgers team. In the 1950s, white players were more common and accepted.

Clemente had been excited to move to Brooklyn. A lot of Spanish-speaking people lived there, and many of them were from Puerto Rico. Everything in Montreal—a city in Canada—was strange and difficult. The weather was much colder than it was in Puerto Rico. Plus most people spoke French, and he didn't have many people he could talk to. He was very lonely, still a teenager and living away from home for the first time.

Clemente's life was full of new experiences. One of the most upsetting was his first exposure to prejudice. In Puerto Rico, the color of a person's skin had never seemed important. But when the Royals traveled to places in the southern part of the United States, the black players were not allowed to stay in the same hotels or eat in the same restaurants.

But he loved baseball and thought that as long as he had the chance to play, he would be able to overcome the hardships he found in Montreal. Unfortunately, he found himself on the bench much more than on the field. The Dodgers supposedly didn't want any other team to realize what a good player they had, so Clemente didn't get to play very often.

Life & Career Skills

Throughout his long career in baseball, Clemente was often injured or suffered from illness, had to deal with prejudice, and was often lonely. But he never gave up. He stayed focused and continued to work hard through these problems and disappointments.

The Pittsburgh Pirates drafted Clemente (second from left) in 1954.

The Dodgers were worried they would lose Clemente. There was a rule in Major League Baseball that a rookie had to play on his regular team if he received a bonus of more than $4,000. If he played on a farm team, the player could be picked by another team during a special draft. This rule had been created to keep the teams that had more money from keeping all the good players for themselves. The Dodgers had paid Clemente $10,000 and sent him to Montreal. They were taking a big risk!

The draft was set up so that the worst team had the first choice when it came to picking players. That year, the worst team was the Pittsburgh Pirates. And they did, indeed, have their eyes on Clemente. The Pirates' general manager, Branch Rickey, had his scouts watching Clemente. They liked what they saw and were waiting for their chance to draft him.

Clemente didn't know about the Dodgers' plans. All he knew was that he wasn't playing very often, no matter how well he did. He was so angry that he almost quit the Royals. Howie Haak, a scout for the Pirates, came to see Clemente and told him that if he left Montreal before the season was over, he wouldn't be allowed to play for another team. Haak convinced Clemente to finish the season so that Pittsburgh could draft him.

On November 22, 1954, Pittsburgh added Clemente to its team. After years of losing more than 100 games a season, Pittsburgh was working hard to build a better team. The Pirates believed that Clemente might be able to help them do just that.

The Pirates' home field, Forbes Field, was a challenge to Clemente. It was a larger field than he was used to, and he decided that he wouldn't worry about hitting home runs; instead, he'd perfect his line drives. He also worried about fielding balls off the right field walls at Forbes, which were oddly shaped and covered with ivy. He practiced for hours and eventually knew just how a ball would fall depending on where it hit the wall.

21st Century Content

Clemente had an amazing career in baseball, especially considering his many injuries and illnesses. He severely injured his leg, had multiple surgeries on his elbow, had serious back problems, and had malaria. Clemente always looked for solutions to relieve his many pains. He did special exercises and was very careful about what he ate. In the off-season one year, he even went and trained with the U.S. Marine Corps! The difficult workouts helped him to be stronger and to feel better.

Though he faced many difficulties off the field, Clemente (crossing home plate) was amazingly successful on it.

Life off the field was a struggle, too. Clemente often experienced prejudice. The 1950s were not an easy time to be a person of color in the United States. Schools had only been **desegregated** since 1954, and it had been less than 10 years since the first person of color, Jackie Robinson, had been signed to a Major League team. There were very few black or Latin American people in Pittsburgh and Clemente was both, which made his life even more difficult. In the United States, he was viewed as a black man because of the color of his skin, but American blacks did not easily accept him because he came from another country. When Clemente first moved to Pittsburgh, he lived in a hotel. He missed his family and life on the island of Puerto Rico. A friend found a family for him to live with. They were warm and welcoming and helped Clemente adapt to life in the United States.

Life on the road was even more difficult, especially when they traveled in the South. Spring training was held in Florida, a state that was extremely segregated. Sometimes Clemente was not even allowed to attend events that honored the Pittsburgh Pirates because of the color of his skin. The other black players told him to ignore these injustices, but Clemente wouldn't. He had been raised to be proud of his heritage and didn't believe it was right to ignore prejudice.

Back home in Puerto Rico, Clemente was famous and people looked up to him. But in the United States, he was often treated poorly because he was black. To make matters worse, he also faced prejudice because he was from Puerto Rico. Although he worked hard to improve his English, many sportswriters thought it was funny to pick on his pronunciation and grammar mistakes. Others accused him of "hotdogging," or showing off. In fact, one writer described him as a "Puerto Rican hot dog" before he had even seen Clemente play. Clemente was upset that people believed certain things about him based on where he was from and the color of his skin, and he worked hard to prove that people were wrong to judge him because of these things.

Clemente also ran into problems with his own team. Even if players didn't call him names to his face, some of them made negative comments

about other black players. Clemente knew that they probably felt the same about him.

Clemente knew that he could prove himself on the baseball field. He played well during his first seasons with the Pirates, but not as well as he wanted to. He became known for trying to hit every ball that came his way. Pitchers realized this and would throw bad pitches just to strike him out. Over time, Clemente realized that he needed to be more careful about the hits that he tried to make. Although Clemente sometimes disappointed his fans with his batting in the early years, he was never a disappointment in the outfield. The fans knew they could count on Clemente for an exciting game.

As the years passed, he often felt discouraged, but he never stopped trying to improve both his own baseball skills and the performance of his team. In 1960, his hard work paid off. He helped his team to win its first National League **pennant** in 33 years, and, in an exciting seven-game series, the Pittsburgh Pirates became that year's World Series champions.

Though Clemente had an outstanding season, he still didn't think he was completely accepted by sportswriters. Baseball writers from across the country select the National League's Most Valuable

A fellow Pirate, Dick Groat once said that Clemente (sliding)
"was the greatest . . . talent I ever saw on a baseball diamond."

Player (MVP), an award given to the player who has contributed the most
to his team during the season. He was ranked eighth in the voting, and
though he didn't expect to win the MVP, he was surprised and hurt by his
low ranking. He believed that he had given his best to his team and that his
efforts hadn't been appreciated. In fact, no one ever saw Clemente wear the
ring that the Pittsburgh players received for winning the 1960 World Series.

Clemente decided to prove that the sportswriters were wrong.

CHAPTER FOUR

BECOMING A TEAM AND COMMUNITY LEADER

Clemente regularly made spectacular catches in the outfield.

Clemente continued to play his best for Pittsburgh. Although the team didn't go to the World Series the next year, he ended the season with a .351 batting average. Usually anything higher than .300 is good, and a .400 for an entire season is almost impossible to achieve. In 1961, he made the All-Star team for the first time. Players, coaches, and managers chose the members of the All-Star team. They knew he was one of the league's best players.

It was a good year for Clemente in other ways, too. He won his first Gold Glove, an award that recognizes excellent defensive play in the field. He also won the first batting title of his career. When he returned to Puerto Rico after the regular season ended, he and fellow Puerto Rican Orlando Cepeda, who played for the New York Giants, were welcomed by thousands of cheering fans at the airport.

That year, Clemente played in the Winter League in Puerto Rico, as he did almost every year he was in the Major Leagues. The Winter League had became less popular as Major League salaries went up and players didn't need to earn extra money, but he never stopped playing in the Winter League. He thought that this was a way to thank the Puerto Rican people for their support. He returned to the island every year, and he had a very strong connection with the people who lived there.

In 1963, he was especially glad that he returned for the Winter League because that was the year he met his future wife, Vera Cristina Zabala. She came from a very traditional Puerto Rican family. Clemente could not just ask her out; he had to be

Clemente would dive or jump for a ball, and once he even ran into a wall and hurt himself badly going after a ball—but he made the catch! Plus, he had a very powerful arm. As broadcaster Vin Scully once said, "Clemente could field a ball in Pennsylvania and throw out a runner in New York." Though Clemente was naturally talented, he worked tirelessly to improve his already outstanding skills. In recognition of his skill in the outfield, he was given the Gold Glove Award 12 times. This award is given to nine players from each of the two baseball leagues, the National League and the American League, every year.

introduced through family connections. They even had a chaperone on their first date. But Clemente understood and respected the wishes of her family and they came to see that he truly loved her. Clemente and Zabala were engaged and married within a year, and over the next few years they had three sons: Roberto Jr., Luis, and Enrique. All three boys were born in Puerto Rico because Clemente was very proud of his heritage and wanted his children to be Puerto Rican.

It was during these years that Clemente began to become a leader for the Pittsburgh Pirates. Maybe it was because of his happy home life or because there were more Latino players on the team—or because his fellow players had come to appreciate what an excellent, hardworking ballplayer he was. In 1966, the Pirates' manager gave Clemente a challenge: to focus on being a power hitter to help his team. He asked Clemente to try to hit 25 home runs and have 115 **runs batted in** or RBIs. This would be quite a feat because Clemente had never had more than 20 home runs or 100 RBIs in a season. But Clemente was never one to pass up a challenge. He worked hard and by the end of the season he had 29 home runs and 119 RBIs. This was nearly three times as many home runs and twice as many RBIs as he'd had the previous season. In 1966, Clemente signed a $100,000 contract to play for the Pirates—he was one of the few baseball players to earn this much money.

After 10 long years of proving himself, Clemente was voted National League MVP in 1966. This proved that Clemente's abilities and commitment were recognized by people beyond his team and the city of Pittsburgh. He felt proud to be recognized for his achievements and knew

Clemente received the 1965 National League batting champion award.

that he was a role model and inspiration for many other people, especially people of color.

Clemente was more than just an excellent ballplayer to the young Latino players on the team, especially those who were new to the United States. He was a friend and, in many ways, like a big brother. Clemente remembered how difficult and lonely his adjustment to life in a new country had been. He went out of his way to make life easier for the new players and their families.

Clemente helped them to learn English and to find a place to live. He helped them to fit in. He became a close friend and adviser to Manny Mota, who came to Pittsburgh from the Dominican Republic (Mota later went on to be a coach with the Los Angeles Dodgers). Clemente also helped Matty Alou to improve his hitting, working with him for hours and giving him valuable advice. His efforts really paid off. In 1966 Alou was the best batter in the National League. Clemente also befriended Manny Sanguillen, a player from Panama who had always looked up to him.

In both Puerto Rico and Pittsburgh, Clemente became known as a man who always made time to help others, especially children. He visited hospitals and clinics and began to raise money to build a sports center for children in Puerto Rico. He strongly believed that sports could make an important difference in a child's life and wanted to give all children the chance to discover it. In the mid-1960s, he held baseball clinics for poor children in Puerto Rico. It was the first step toward achieving his dream of giving all children the chance to play sports.

Perhaps one of the most important ways that he helped others was by not tolerating prejudice. He knew that many people thought Latino baseball players

Even away from the ballpark, Clemente made time for fans.

weren't as good as white ones. Clemente worked hard to prove them wrong, both on the baseball field and in everyday life. He always spoke proudly of his Puerto Rican heritage and asked to be called by his true name, Roberto, instead of a more American-sounding name like Bob or Bobby.

Unfortunately, Clemente continued to experience prejudice. Once he and his wife went into an expensive furniture store in New York City. Because Clemente was black, the clerk assumed that he could not afford

Clemente was very popular in Pittsburgh.

the nice furniture, and he began to show the Clementes cheaper furniture. When the clerk realized that the man in front of him was a famous baseball star, he began to treat him respectfully. Clemente was extremely angry and told the clerk that everyone should be treated the same, regardless of their skin color or where they came from. He refused to buy anything and left the store.

Even after a hard game, Clemente was never too tired to talk to his fans and sign autographs. He said, "I sign 20,000 autographs a year. . . . I believe that we owe something to the people who watch us. They work hard for their money."

The fans loved him and cheered when it was his turn to play. They knew that once he took to the field, they could expect to see an exciting game. In fact, he was so popular with Pittsburgh fans that shortly after the team moved to a new stadium in 1970, they held Roberto Clemente Night. During the celebration, he received a scroll that listed the signatures of more than 300,000 people from the island of Puerto Rico. Clemente was overcome with emotion as he spoke to the audience. He spoke of his success in baseball as a success not just for him, but for all Latinos and dedicated his efforts to all Puerto Rican mothers, athletes, and his family.

Clemente continued to be one of the best players in the Major Leagues, even though he was older than many of the people he played with and against. In 1971, he again helped to take the Pittsburgh Pirates to the World Series. Although their opponents, the Baltimore Orioles, were expected to win the series, Clemente knew that his team had the ability—and the desire—to beat them.

During the series, he played some of the best baseball of his career. He batted .414, and his excellent fielding helped the Pirates to win the series. Sportswriters recognized Clemente's efforts and talents and gave him

Clemente had four 200-hit seasons.

the series MVP award. As he accepted the award on television, he shared a special message with his parents back in Puerto Rico, "En este, el momento más grande de mi vida, les pido la bendición" ("At this, the greatest moment of my life, I ask your blessing").

CHAPTER FIVE

THE BEGINNING OF A LEGEND

Clemente played 18 seasons with the Pittsburgh Pirates.

In 1972, Clemente was 38 years old. He had been a professional baseball player for more than half of his life, and his skill and hard work had finally been recognized. But he had one more important goal to achieve in his

On September 30, 1972, Clemente's double against the Mets became his 3,000th hit. The umpire handed Clemente the ball he had hit.

career: he wanted to get 3,000 hits. At that time, only 10 Major League players had reached that goal. Roberto knew he could be the 11th.

At the beginning of the 1972 baseball season, Clemente still needed 118 hits. Throughout the season, he struggled with injuries, and his fans waited anxiously as he approached his goal during that summer. Finally, on September 29, 1972, he had 2,999 hits. In an exciting game against the New York Mets, he achieved what he thought would be his 3,000th hit. He was on base, but the player who had fielded the ball made an error. A batter reaching base on a fielder's error does not receive credit for a hit.

At first, he was angry and frustrated, but he later said that he was glad the scorer didn't call the ball a hit. He didn't want anyone to be able to say that his 3,000th hit shouldn't count.

Then on September 30, 1972, Clemente made his 3,000th hit. He became the first Latin American player to reach this milestone.

The Pittsburgh Pirates lost in the **play-offs** to the Cincinnati Reds, and their season was over. Clemente returned to Puerto Rico to rest and enjoy time with his family and friends, but his rest didn't last for long. On December 23, 1972, a terrible earthquake struck the country of Nicaragua, which is located in Central America. Although Clemente didn't have any close ties to the country, he had visited it recently and wanted to help the Nicaraguans. He quickly agreed to be in charge of Puerto Rico's efforts to collect money, food, and supplies for those affected by the earthquake.

Clemente worked tirelessly to gather goods and get them to the people of Nicaragua. When he learned that many of the donated items were not reaching the people who needed them, he decided to

21st Century Content

Roberto's Kids is an organization that collects donated baseball equipment from the United States and Canada and gives it to children in Latin American countries. As Luis Clemente, Roberto's youngest son said, "Roberto's Kids, . . . in the Clemente tradition of giving and caring for others, . . . is truly making a difference by touching and inspiring so many lives."

Clemente was inducted into the Baseball Hall of Fame in 1973.

travel to Nicaragua himself. He would make sure that the supplies were delivered safely.

Unfortunately, he never made it to Nicaragua. His plane left from San Juan on December 31, 1972, but it soon developed engine trouble and crashed into the ocean.

People all over Puerto Rico mourned their lost hero, a man who proudly represented his country and heritage and tirelessly devoted his time to those less fortunate. The country's new governor postponed his inauguration while boats and divers searched for Clemente. One of the divers was Manny Sanguillen, the Panamanian baseball player who had come to view Clemente as an older brother. But Clemente's body was never found. On January 4, 1973, a church in Pittsburgh and the church where Clemente and his wife had been married, San Fernando Church in Carolina, held Mass at the same time so that his family, friends, and many fans could grieve for him together.

Two months later, baseball writers held a special election and voted that Clemente should be inducted into the Baseball Hall of Fame immediately. Baseball players usually have to wait until five years after they've played their last game to be eligible to be inducted. Clemente was the first Latin American player to join the Baseball Hall of Fame. To honor one of their best players, the Pittsburgh Pirates retired Clemente's number, 21.

Major League Baseball also honored him. In 1971, the organization had created an annual award to recognize the baseball player who gave back the most to his community. After Clemente's death, the owners changed the name of the award to the Roberto Clemente Award. It was extremely fitting that those who worked hard to make the world a better place would be recognized with an award named after a man who had always tried to do just that.

Communities around the world recognized Clemente by naming public places after him. Today, there are schools, parks, bridges, and ballparks named after him throughout the United States and Puerto Rico, as well as in several other countries.

One of the most important ways that people honored him was by donating money to fund one of his most cherished dreams: a sports center, Ciudad Deportiva, in San Juan, Puerto Rico. The island of Puerto Rico

donated the land that the center now stands on. Because of this center, thousands of Puerto Rican children have had the chance to discover the joys of playing sports.

Even though his death was more than 30 years ago, his presence is still felt in baseball and beyond. A statue of Clemente stands outside the Pirates' stadium in Pittsburgh, and the city renamed a bridge after him in 1999. In 2002, Major League Baseball's commissioner, Allan H. (Bud) Selig, announced that September 18 would be celebrated as Roberto Clemente Day among all Major League teams.

In 2003, President George W. Bush awarded Clemente the Presidential Medal of Freedom, which his widow, Vera Clemente, accepted. This is the United States' highest civilian award and is given to recognize a person's exceptional service.

And in 2006, the people of Pittsburgh continued to remember "The Great One," as he came to be known. On July 13, 2006, when Pittsburgh hosted the All-Star Game, his widow accepted the Commissioner's Historic Achievement Award in his honor. During the game, players wore gold wristbands monogrammed with RCW—Roberto Clemente Walker.

In 2006, Carlos Delgado received the Roberto Clemente Award for his charitable work.

Today, Latin American baseball players and other players of color are a common sight on the baseball field. They owe Roberto Clemente a debt of thanks for helping to make their journey to Major League Baseball easier.

But being a wonderful baseball player was only part of who Roberto Clemente was. People of every color, race, and ethnic group can learn

A statue of Clemente stands outside the stadium where the Pirates play today.

from the lessons that he shared during his short lifetime: respect others, work hard, stand up for what you believe in, and always do what you can to make the world a better place. "We need to show love and to love, not only our kids and our family as a whole, but also our neighbors. We're all brothers and sisters, and we must give each other a helping hand when it is needed."

Manny Sanguillen, a teammate and good friend of Clemente's, once said, "Roberto Clemente played the game of baseball with great passion. That passion could only be matched by his unrelenting commitment to make a difference in the lives of the less fortunate and those in need."

Dr. Martin Luther King Jr. led the civil rights movement in the United States from the mid-1950s until he was assassinated in 1968. Through the marches and demonstrations he organized and speeches he gave, he promoted equal rights for all and inspired others to do the same. Clemente greatly admired King and shared King's views that no people should be discriminated against because of the color of their skin.

Timeline

1934 Roberto Clemente Walker is born August 18 to Melchor and Luisa Clemente in Carolina, Puerto Rico.

1952 Clemente joins the Santurce Cangrejeros of the Winter League.

1954 Clemente signs a contract with the Brooklyn Dodgers and plays for their farm team, the Montreal Royals.

1955 Clemente plays his first season with the Pittsburgh Pirates.

1960 The Pittsburgh Pirates win the World Series against the New York Yankees.

1961 Clemente wins his first Gold Glove Award for fielding and his first batting title, and makes the All-Star team.

1964 Clemente marries Vera Zabala; he wins his second batting title.

1965 Clemente wins his third batting title.

1966 Clemente is voted the National League's Most Valuable Player.

1967 Clemente wins his fourth batting title.

1970 Pittsburgh moves to a new stadium and holds Roberto Clemente Night.

1971 The Pirates defeat the Baltimore Orioles in the World Series; Clemente is selected Most Valuable Player for the series.

1972 Clemente collects his 3,000th hit. He dies in a plane crash on December 31 while bringing supplies to Nicaragua.

1973 Clemente is elected to the Baseball Hall of Fame; Pittsburgh retires his number, 21.

1984   The U.S. Post Office unveils a Roberto Clemente stamp on the 50th anniversary of his birth.

1994   A statue of Clemente is erected at Three Rivers Stadium.

2002   Major League Baseball announces and celebrates the first Roberto Clemente Day on September 18.

2003   Clemente is awarded the Presidential Medal of Freedom.

2006   Clemente is awarded the Commissioner's Historic Achievement Award during the All-Star Game in Pittsburgh.

GLOSSARY

batting average (BAT-ting AV-uh-rij) the number of hits that a player has made, divided by the number of times he's had a turn at bat

desegregated (dee-SEG-ruh-gay-ted) to stop the practice of keeping people of different races separate, especially in public schools

discriminated (diss-KRIM-uh-nay-ted) to be treated differently, often on the basis of sex, race, religion, or ethnic group

draft (DRAFT) to choose for a special purpose; in this case, to choose a player for a baseball team

farm team (FARM TEEM) a team that provides experience and training to younger players for a specific Major League team

Latin American (LAT-uhn um-MER-uh-kuhn) usually refers to the countries in the Americas where the Spanish and Portuguese languages are spoken

line drives (LINE DRYVZ) hits that go in a nearly straight line, usually not far above the ground

Major Leagues (MAY-jur LEEGS) professional baseball in the United States. There are two leagues within it: the National League and the American League.

Negro Leagues (NEE-groh LEEGS) separate professional baseball leagues for black players that existed because black players were not allowed to play in the Major Leagues

pennant (PEN-uhnt) the league championship

play-offs (PLAY AWFS) a series of games to determine which teams will play in the World Series

prejudice (PREJ-uh-diss) unfair treatment that results from having fixed opinions about some group of people

rival (RYE-vuhl) a competitor

runs batted in (RUHNZ BA-tuhd IN) each run scored because of a batter's performance

scout (SKOUT) watching athletes, analyzing their skills, and reporting back to a specific team

Winter League (WIN-tur LEEG) a professional baseball league in Puerto Rico that played during the winter months

FOR MORE INFORMATION

Books

Bjarkman, Peter C. *Roberto Clemente*. New York: Chelsea House Publishers, 1991.

Dunham, Montrew. *Roberto Clemente: Young Ball Player*.
New York: Aladdin Paperbacks, 1997.

Márquez, Herón. *Roberto Clemente: Baseball's Humanitarian
Hero*. Minneapolis, MN: Carolrhoda Books, 2005

O'Connor, Jim. *The Story of Roberto Clemente, All-Star Hero*.
Milwaukee, WI: Gareth Stevens Publishing, 1995.

Web Sites

Major League Baseball: Roberto Clemente Award
mlb.mlb.com/mlb/official_info/community/clemente.jsp
For information about the award, including nominees and winners

**Smithsonian Institution Traveling Exhibition Service
Beyond Baseball: The Life of Roberto Clemente**
www.robertoclemente.si.edu/english/virtual_legacy.htm
Includes a biography, images, and interactive games

The Pittsburgh Pirates
pittsburgh.pirates.mlb.com
Features statistics, rosters, history, and more about the Pirates

INDEX

ABOUT THE AUTHOR

Vicky Franchino has always liked to learn about people who have made a difference in the world. Before writing this book she knew very little about Roberto Clemente, but she now understands why people still remember and honor him more than 30 years after his death. She hopes Clemente's story will help to inspire others to use their talents and time to make the world a better place. Vicky is the author of a number of other nonfiction books for children, and lives with her husband and their three daughters in Wisconsin.